Modern Floral

For John Graham.
Thank you for your love, support and friendship, and for your
guidance towards our custodianship of Marnanie.

CHARLOTTE COOTE

Modern Floral

TIMELESS INTERIORS INSPIRED
BY NATURE

Contents

FOREWORD BY INDIA HICKS – 6 –

INTRODUCTION – 9 –

CHAPTER 01
THE DESIGNER'S EYE
– 15 –

CHAPTER 02
BOTANICALS THROUGH THE AGES
– 39 –

CHAPTER 03
DESIGNING WITH FLORAL TEXTILES
– 65 –

CHAPTER 04
ANTIQUE TEXTILES
– 99 –

CHAPTER 05
USING COLOURS FROM NATURE
– 115 –

CHAPTER 06
INTRODUCING NATURAL TEXTILES
– 167 –

CHAPTER 07
WORKING WITH FLOWERS AND GREENERY
– 189 –

ART CREDITS – 222 –

ACKNOWLEDGEMENTS – 223 –

Foreword

BY
INDIA HICKS

If Charlotte Coote had one spare moment in her life, what do you think she would be doing with it? Certainly not lying down with her feet up. She'd be walking dogs, running the kids to school, tackling a tricky client, plumping a cushion, but most probably she'd be in her flower room arranging some spectacular display in a gigantic, oversized vase. I've been in Charlotte's flower room, in her home Marnanie, and it's as spectacular as her interior design projects, a room you want to linger in, a room with history.

I also have history with Charlotte, our fathers were great friends and great rivals, teasing each other rotten from Ireland to England and Australia. Both men were opinionated, outspoken and very sure of their likes and dislikes. My father had a list of 'unacceptable flowers'. Dahlias and delphiniums topped the list but later in his life he decided that even the poor old daffodil was considered the wrong shade of yellow.

Charlotte is softer in her approach but no less informed that our dynamic dads. It comes as no surprise that this book travels well beyond the flower room, taking us on a journey of colour, shape, pattern and movement, all carefully brought together by a remarkable leader in interior design.

Introduction

The interiors that have always stayed with me are, more often than not, those that feel confident. They unashamedly exist in their unique authenticity and beauty. The best rooms are those that don't seek your approval. They are quietly confident in their own strength and existence, drawing you to spend time within the promise of their walls. It's no different to spending time with a confident friend or being within a majestic landscape; you immediately feel happy, at home and inspired. I think a room should always aim to provide this at some level. No greater confidence can be offered than the timelessness and elegance of the outside world. To be constantly reminded of the shapes, patterns or cyclical movement provided by nature is a strong and grounding foundation from which to create. It promises happiness, peace and clarity. It anchors. And it is therefore the first place I often look to for inspiration in designing strong, timeless interiors for my clients.

We are all born with a deep connection to the world that surrounds us. Through the ages and across cultures, the outside world has been joyfully celebrated in our interiors. Around 3000 BCE, the Minoan civilisation in what is now Crete famously painted frescoes with elaborate dancing lilies that celebrated the arrival of spring. The ancient Egyptian tomb of Sennefer in Luxor, circa 1300 BCE, is beautifully decorated with an arbour of vines.

The natural world inspires, informs and influences our homes and can create a sense of joy and harmony around us. Natural materials like stone, wood, linen and jute in our homes create a grounded feeling. Expansive windows give us unobstructed views of the natural world. We even create indoor gardens. And then there are the textiles that tie everything together and bring interiors to life – fabulous designs inspired by flora, fauna and botanicals. The textiles featured in this book have inspired and informed my own work as a designer, helping me bring the beauty of the natural surroundings into my interiors.

Chintz and botanical-inspired textiles have been around for over 500 years, adorning both our homes and wardrobes. Successful designers have

OPPOSITE – *This country dining room was inspired by its leafy environment. The earthy colours are drawn from the flora and fauna outside the window and the hearty texture of the wool walls creates depth and warmth. The wood, linen, wool rug and Murano glass leaf chandelier in this sophisticated dining room speak subtly of nature.*

FOLLOWING – *I find endless inspiration in my garden at Marnanie. Working with antique textiles in the streamhouse brings me great joy.*

INTRODUCTION

committed to them in the past and present, rescuing and reinventing them along the way. They may go in and out of vogue, but they never seem to lie dormant for long. In fact, their reinterpretation and re-emergence only strengthen their timelessness.

It is interesting is to observe how modern style makers and designers continue to take inspiration from past designs and reimagine them for the present. Scottish textile house Timorous Beasties, for example, are recognised for their unique and contemporary nature-inspired designs. Their designers have cleverly adapted the classic toile to create entirely new scenes and stories of contemporary Edinburgh, Glasgow and London. The shift is away from the typical historic design, instead reinterpreting the iconic motifs to bring them into the modern era. These designs won't appeal to everyone, but's that's the whole point.

An aesthetic is rarely, if ever, an entirely original concept. Usually at least one element is borrowed from elsewhere. I often reference another era or an iconic designer in my own work. I look to bygone designers and products for inspiration, then allow the ideas to inform my own interiors and products. A refreshing new take is needed and authenticity is key.

More than ever, we should be looking to nature for inspiration and to counteract the often chaotic, unnatural spaces we inhabit. At the beginning of any design project – especially my own – the outside world is often the first place I look to for that initial creative spark.

It's where the concept of my own flower room and kitchen began. It's informed every event my husband and I have hosted at our home, Marnanie. It's also where we found our inspiration for the Tasmanian beach house project we are currently working on with my team.

A clever photographer once told me that, if I really observed what was in front of me, I could capture something both interesting and authentic. In this book, I will walk you through this process and provide examples of interiors I have created using this method. I hope it inspires you.

OPPOSITE – *This light-filled corner with its leafy outlook is an ideal spot for a cup of tea and a book. I kept the furnishings simple – green and neutral tones and contrasting textures of velvet, wool and glazed linen.*

ABOVE – *Working with piles of antique chintz.*

The Designer's Eye

CHAPTER 01

It's not what you look at that matters, it's what you see.

– Henry David Thoreau

The Designer's Eye

How to know what to see is a valuable skill. Some people are born with a great eye for design, but I believe it can also be learned and honed with experience and exposure. The ability to spot beauty in all its forms, where others do not, is a valuable skill. It could be perfectly placing an object, noticing an unexpected but delightful colour combination in an interior, or choosing an exceptional antique textile over the ordinary ones at a Paris flea market.

VISITING THE ALHAMBRA in Granada, Spain, recently I had a completely different experience to my first visit there twenty years ago. Yet it was the same place. Perhaps my life experience has given me a greater appreciation of its history or more confidence in my own eye. Maybe my design knowledge also contributed.

To notice more, to see more, you must sharpen your sixth sense and trust your intuition. Even when you see something that, at first glance, seems quite simple, don't immediately disregard it. It might inspire a hugely interesting idea.

Being completely present with what is in front of you and understanding what sets it apart and why it interests you is enormously useful. Remember, what you see and what others see will always be different. That is the beauty of intuition and the power of your unique designer's eye.

Colour

When I travel, colour often catches my eye, inspiring me to photograph objects and scenes. It can be anything – the way a vibrant bougainvillea contrasts with the faded painted wall it shades, or the still vivid pigment of a 13th-century Moorish tile.

I NOTICE THE world around me more intensely when I travel, and this strongly influences the creation of future ideas. There is always the potential for a wonderful surprise around the next corner. And there are many more colours in the real world than those you find in a paint chart. Nature brings unexpected colours together, and it always works. Make sure to seek out unique flora and fauna when you travel – you will see entirely different species and colours than you do at home.

Pay attention to understated colours, too. There can be great beauty in subtlety. I loved the bespoke colour – Polish Grey – of the original shutters at Amangalla in Galle, Sri Lanka. I was also inspired by the sunburnt colour of homes in the Kasbah in Tangier, Morocco.

Like everything in life, the more you practise using your eye, the better you will become at it. The more you notice and experience how colour is used, the more sophisticated and confident you will be when you are creating with it.

Pattern and Shape

The way shapes exist and interact with each other fascinates me and plays a huge role in the way I create. There is importance to the individual form and proportion of an object as well as its scale and how it is arranged with other objects. Get this right and you can turn a previously unremarkable space into something fabulous.

THERE ARE INTERESTING patterns and shapes everywhere: tessellating tiles, geometric rugs, repeating architectural elements, sculpted hedges and painted motifs. Interesting patterns can be found in unusual places, like the repeating Y-shape in steel electrical covers on old footpaths in Europe and India. These could inspire the design of a rug for a future project.

The shapes created by architecture are also endlessly interesting and inspiring. Look out for archways, pillars, banisters, railings or intricate ceiling designs. These details can make a space sing but they can also be reimagined to design furniture or provide a pattern for soft furnishings.

Design Details and Finishing Touches

Often it's the tiniest details that define the most impressive creations. Think of the shape and patina of interesting door hardware or the profile of a hand-carved table. Consider how the repetition of a tile anchors a room or the way a trim enhances a cushion or curtain. A collection of antique plates might provide an authentic way to style a wall. An arrangement of objects can perfectly finish a table.

EVEN SOMETHING AS small as a typeface can transform the appearance of a building. I was particularly drawn to the font used on Tangier's iconic cinemas. Their colour and personality reminded me of a Wes Anderson scene. They beckoned to me, inviting me in to watch a film. I also adore collecting antique monogrammed linen. I love the way that the forms of the lettering can elevate and personalise a table and make it more interesting.

Painted Details

There is something infinitely charming about a handpainted object. Perhaps it's the time and skill that were required to create it, or an appreciation of the unique eye of the artist. Beautifully handpainted furniture, lampshades, wallpapers, doors and ceramics can add authenticity and an artisanal element to your space, setting it apart.

PAINTING AN OLD or existing object can also give it an entirely new lease on life. I am fortunate to have been to the studio of the Spanish-born, London-based creator of handpainted lampshades, Alvaro Picardo. I have also visited the ceramic and textile producers at The Exvotos in Seville, Spain, and many other artisans.

Seeing how these craftspeople create their wares gave me a greater appreciation for the dedication, expertise and visual acuity that go into producing each piece. No two creations are the same – each is a unique extension of its maker.

A friend once introduced me to an old man in Seville who makes his own marbled paper and uses it to create leather-bound visitors' books. The paper was exquisite. Sadly, he refused to sell me any of his paper. He didn't care about the money; he was worried that the paper would be damaged in transit. Instead, he allowed me to buy some of his books. Never underestimate the pride and skill that go into anything made by hand!

Natural Fibres and Textures

Bamboo, stone, wood, linen, wool, wicker, silk, resin, cane, rope and sisal are all natural fibres and textures I love to work with. Every country has its own unique collection of natural resources that result in materials and textures that are not seen anywhere else. When I am visiting a new country, I always attempt to find out what raw materials the local artisans are using. They are usually something unique to the area, with a long tradition behind them.

INVESTIGATING DIFFERENT MATERIALS and techniques can lead you to think about how you might use different resources, or how you could use familiar resources differently.

CHAPTER 01 – THE DESIGNER'S EYE

My Favourite Botanical Textiles

COLEFAX AND FOWLER 'BOWOOD'

ONE OF MY go-to choices for interiors, 'Bowood' is a classic chintz textile that was inspired by an original document originally found by John Fowler at Bowood House, a historic Georgian country house in Wiltshire, England.

First produced in 1964, 'Bowood' chintz was inspired by John Fowler's visit to Bowood House during the 1950s while he was decorating the interiors for the Marchioness of Lansdowne. It is still available as both a wallpaper and textile.

I love the timelessness of 'Bowood'. It is pretty and feminine, yet simple and repetitive. It could be used in a fresh, contemporary interior. Unlike many chintz textiles, it isn't chaotic or challenging. It isn't old-fashioned either, but it is reminiscent of old-world glamour and is easy to use and build from.

CHAPTER 01 — THE DESIGNER'S EYE

JEAN MONRO: 'BRIAR ROSE'

THE 'BRIAR ROSE' wallpaper was inspired by antique curtains found in a house in Kingsbridge, England. To further balance the English design, the Jean Monro team added briar roses and blackberries between the main bunch of flowers.

The Coote & Co. team and I used this wallpaper as the hero of an interior design window. We were drawn to its lovely aqua background and the fresh vibrant pinks, white and greens. The challenge was to reinvent the textile without it feeling daggy or old-fashioned. Each element in the window relates to, or balances, the wallpaper to create a fresh and interesting new take.

DESIGNING AROUND 'BRIAR ROSE'

1. The stunning blues of Cathy Carter's archival print, Icebergs 2018.

2. The woody stems in the wallpaper were complemented by the terracotta pots, antique timber shutters, handmade Murano glass shell sconce, wicker trays and wicker handbag.

3. Handpainted geometric lampshades by Alvaro Picardo in a mustard colour added structure.

4. A contemporary 1980s travertine console with art deco angles balances the organic motif of the wallpaper and brings in a natural material.

5. A contemporary Perspex chess set by Karim Rashid added fun, life and something unusual. It offset the pretty floral background while mimicking its colours.

6. The antique French red-and-white striped occasional chair provided a bold contrast to the pastels. The persimmons and red bottles helped tie it in with the space.

7. The aqua of the ottoman and Cathy Carter's print reflected the background of the wallpaper.

Botanicals Through the Ages

CHAPTER 02

If you want a
new idea, read
an old book.

– Ivan Pavlov

Botanicals Through the Ages

More and more people are seeking a connection to nature and reminders of the outside world in their homes. I often look to the outdoors when I am planning interiors, parties or events and think about what natural colours, patterns, florals, wildlife or materials I can bring into what I'm creating. It is a wonderful place to begin.

I ALSO LOVE including botanical prints when I am creating textile schemes. They create a story and bring movement and a certain dreaminess to my designs. Our lives are enhanced when we are exposed to the outside world. Being constantly reminded of nature – whether explicitly or subliminally – makes us happy.

Chintz and botanical-inspired rooms created over the past 100 years still influence modern culture and design and inform many of the decisions made by today's style makers. The following rooms have fascinated and inspired me throughout my career – I hope they will do the same for you.

PREVIOUS AND OPPOSITE – *This country sunroom is adorned with GP & J Baker 'Chifu' wallpaper in Emerald. The fresh green and white brings a contemporary edge to the classic design – it is the perfect backdrop for the cane furniture, travertine and lovely green and white textiles in this space.*

CHAPTER 02 – BOTANICALS THROUGH THE AGES

Chintz

Chintz is an iconic textile that originated in India in the 16th century.

ORIGINALLY, 'CHINTZ' (from the Hindi word 'chint', which means spotted or variegated) referred to calico that had been block-printed, painted or stained and was usually finished with a glazed coating. It was highly favoured for its practical attributes, since it could be literally wiped clean. The designs featured bright, colourful flowers and other botanical patterns on a plain background.

Initially used mostly for curtains, upholstery and bedding, chintz was also embraced in the fashion world, where its beautifully saturated colours and the depth of the pigments made it very popular.

Technically, 'chintz' refers to a glazed cotton. (If the textile is not glazed, it is called a cretonne or a botanical print.) However, the term is used more generally in contemporary language to describe any floral or botanical textile, and we often use it that way throughout this book.

OPPOSITE – *A happy mix of antique textiles.*

The History of Chintz

EARLY 1600S

CHINTZ FIRST ARRIVED in Europe via Hyderadad in south-central India in the early 1600s. The earliest known surviving piece of chintz, however, was found in Egypt's Red Sea ports. It was made in western India in the early 15th century.

2020S

DRIVEN BY MILLENNIALS who are seeking to break the monotony of the Instagram age, a more layered and decorative design approach, including chintz, is returning. This generation is inspired by the designs of Billy Baldwin, Nancy Lancaster and Albert Hadley. It seems that chintz is here to stay.

1990S

THE USE OF chintz came to an abrupt end. Top designers, such as Albert Hadley, instructed their staff to throw out all the chintz samples in their library. Ikea even ran an advertising campaign showing homeowners throwing chintz-covered lampshades out of windows. The 1990s were to be a time of neutrals and sleek, fuss-free interiors.

1980S

THE RE-EMERGENCE OF chintz in the fashion world was largely due to Diana, Princess of Wales, who favoured English-style chintz dresses designed by Laura Ashley. Chintz was also seen in many popular films, including *Risky Business* and *Pretty in Pink*.

MID 1600S

ADORED AND MADE popular by 17th-century European royalty and aristocracy, chintz was a significant textile in the world of interior decoration and fashion. Most commonly, it was used to make bespoke curtains and upholstery.

EARLY 1700S

BOTH THE FRENCH and English governments banned the importation of Indian chintz. The Calico Acts (1700–21) were passed in England to protect the local textile manufacturing industry from India, which dominated global cotton textile markets at the time.

1955

STYLE MAKER AND editor of *Vogue*, Diana Vreeland, made a bold statement in her New York apartment by covering her living room walls and furniture in a scarlet *fleurs du mal* chintz. She used the same fabric, in blue, in her bedroom (see p. 54).

1907

AMERICAN DESIGNER ELSIE de Wolfe gained popularity for her fresh take on interiors that prioritised comfort and space over the cluttered interiors of the Victorian era. She favoured soft colour palettes and an abundance of glazed chintz (see p. 53).

LATE 1800S

IN 1876 THE East India Company reported that their profits from exporting cloth to Europe had finally surpassed their profits from exporting spices. Chintz was the first Western love affair with Indian textiles.

CHAPTER 02 – BOTANICALS THROUGH THE AGES

Schumacher: A Botanical History

SCHUMACHER IS AN American family-owned textile house that was founded in 1889 by Paris-born Frederic Schumacher. He started the business in New York, a city brimming with prosperity and opportunity. The brand quickly became famous for supplying high-quality textiles to private residences and luxury hotels such as Park Avenue's Waldorf Astoria.

ABOVE – *This 'Hydrangea' textile, designed by Paul Poiret in 1930, is still in production today.*

TIMELINE

1902

SCHUMACHER IS COMMISSIONED to design and create a floral satin lampas textile for President Roosevelt, who wanted to update the Victorian-era interiors of the White House. The blue and gold lampas is used in the White House for many decades.

1913

AMERICAN DESIGNER ELSIE de Wolfe becomes the first professional interior decorator to support and choose Schumacher textiles. Her career takes off after the success of her designs for New York's Colony Club.

1930

FRENCH DESIGNER PAUL Poiret collaborates with Schumacher to create an iconic range of textiles including 'Hydrangea'. Poiret famously describes himself as 'an artist, not a dressmaker'. Known as the 'King of Fashion', Poiret was one of the first fashion designers to expand and diversify his brand into the world of interior design.

1939

AMERICAN ACTRESS VIVIEN Leigh stars in the iconic film *Gone With the Wind*. The Schumacher 'Hydrangea Drape' wallpaper seen in one of the most famous scenes was created by legendary set designer Hobe Erwin. The pattern is still in production today.

1944

AMERICAN DESIGNER DOROTHY Draper designs the interiors for The Greenbrier hotel using many over-scaled floral textiles, including her iconic 'Manor Rose', which she designed in collaboration with Schumacher.

1947

ACCLAIMED MID-CENTURY VIENNESE designer and architect Josef Frank creates the famous 'Citrus Garden' textile for Schumacher.

1958

DESIGNER ELSA SCHIAPARELLI designs brightly coloured and structured floral and pink textiles in a collaboration with Schumacher.

1962

JACQUELINE KENNEDY GIVES a famous televised tour of the newly renovated White House, including the Blue Room, which is covered entirely with Schumacher's 'Blue Room Lampas' weave.

CHAPTER 02 – BOTANICALS THROUGH THE AGES

INTERVIEW

Lulu Lytle

FOUNDER & CREATIVE DIRECTOR, SOANE BRITAIN

What was the beautiful Egyptian antique textile I saw in Soane Britain March 2023, which inspired your 2023 Soane Britain textile range?

An Egyptian *khayamiya*, which would have been made in Cairo in the 1920s. I have collected these appliqued tent panels for decades, buying my first one when I was fourteen!

How and why did that antique textile inspire the 2023 textile range?

Nearly all Soane's textiles are inspired by antique pieces, some very loosely, perhaps just by a small element of a more detailed pattern or by the structure of a weave, whilst others are more literal – as is the case with the Karun Thakar collaboration relating to the very best Coromandel Coast chintzes.

Your 2024 Soane Britain botanical textile collaboration with Charlotte Johnstone drew on her love of gardens and chintz, which I adore. I note that you also draw from 18th-century textiles like the Reynolds stripe. Do you have an antique collection you reference?

Yes, I have collected textiles since my early teens and we have a very broad archive now at Soane with thousands of pieces, from tiny fragments to very large carpets and wall hangings. The collection spans periods, continents, techniques and fibres, from Coptic Egyptian 4th-century linen and wool weaves to 18th-century Indonesian cotton prints, from Italian ecclesiastical woven velvets to English art deco printed silks.

Was there one other antique textile which has inspired your past textile range? Could you please tell me about why it was special?

It really is hard to narrow this down but perhaps I would say that my Mulhouse pattern books from the 1820s have been a particularly rich source of inspiration.

As a designer, how do you like to reinvent a floral or botanical-inspired interior to stop it from feeling dated or too traditional?

I often strip out many of the elements, making a complex design more graphic. We usually recolour designs, which can immediately breathe new life into an otherwise fusty fabric!

What is your all-time favourite botanical textile?

This is so hard and it really does change all the time. But at the moment I think it would have to be the Coromandel Tulip from our collaboration with Karun, which I recoloured in browns and indigos so it feels like a more sober chintz. We have lined the walls of our New York showroom in this print and I really am in love!

What do you think the future of botanical textiles and the interior will be?

Bountiful! How can you not be seduced by a really well drawn botanical?!

OPPOSITE, CLOCKWISE FROM TOP LEFT — *'Persian Flower, Jewel', 'Filigree Flower, Gilt' 'Jasmine and Frangipani, Walnut and Neel' and 'Trellis Twine, Jamawar'; all by Soane Britain.*

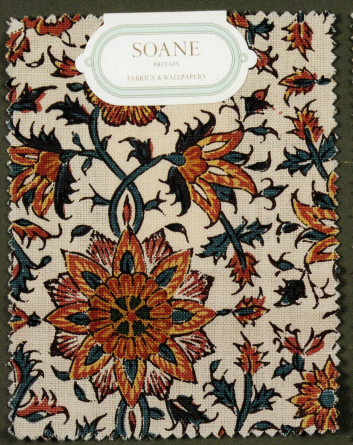

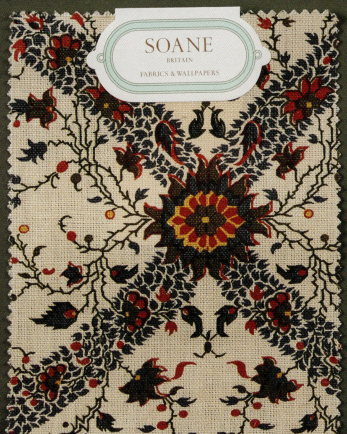

CHAPTER 02 – BOTANICALS THROUGH THE AGES

1907
Elsie de Wolfe: Colony Club Trellis Room

*I'm going to make everything around me beautiful,
that will be my life.*

– Elsie de Wolfe

ONE OF MY favourite botanical-inspired interiors is the Colony Club, a private women's club in New York. It was designed in 1907 by the trailblazing American interior designer Elsie de Wolfe, who famously shunned the heavy textiles, dark palettes and busy furniture of the time in favour of fresh colours, spaciousness and comfort.

Her most iconic room in the Colony Club was the Trellis Room. Her vision was to bring the garden into the space and imbue it with an aura of elegance, femininity and sophistication. She layered the vast room's walls and ceiling with a dark green lattice, so it resembled a freestanding garden pavilion. Elsie was inspired by the 18th-century French treillage she had read about and seen on her travels – by reimagining this idea for the interior of a private 20th-century club she breathed new life into a timeless design classic.

Elsie also brought large working outdoor fountains into the room so that the background sound of trickling water would be a constant reminder of nature. Large-scale hanging lanterns, and cut-off pillars spilling with huge arrangements of flowers, lined the room and double-height French doors opened onto the garden outside.

The Victorian era had not previously seen flowers or furnishings executed in such spectacular scale and proportion. Designers like Elsie and Constance Spry were trailblazers, moving away from the petite and cluttered style of the Victorian era in favour of sparser interiors decorated with generosity and comfort.

Elsie also cleverly used new materials like wicker, cheerfully coloured chintz and botanical textiles, and elegant white tablecloths. She swapped heavy 19th-century Victorian furniture for more-refined antique French pieces, which she mixed with comfortable modern upholstered sofas and oversized armchairs. Intimate spaces were created that were dedicated to conversation.

The concept, which took Elsie almost two years to complete, launched her interior design career. Almost overnight, she gained high-profile clients such as Oscar Wilde and Wallis Simpson, the Duchess of Windsor. Stylish and affluent Colony Club members also saw the brilliance, beauty and originality of her creations and quickly commissioned her to design their own private interiors.

OPPOSITE – *Watercolour interpretation of Elsie de Wolfe's Trellis Room.*

1955
Diana Vreeland: Garden From Hell

A little bad taste is like a nice splash of paprika. We all need a splash of bad taste – it's hearty, it's healthy, it's physical.

– Diana Vreeland

IN 1955, DIANA Vreeland, style maker and former editor-in-chief of *Vogue*, famously teamed up with a good friend, the acclaimed American interior designer Billy Baldwin, to create a red floral sitting room that they dubbed 'The garden from hell'.

Baldwin created a beautifully balanced room. It was completely over the top – to match its larger-than-life inhabitant – but it worked. The furniture layout was considered and comfort was prioritised. And, like all of Baldwin's rooms, it was unashamedly authentic.

The hero of the room was a large-scale scarlet chintz covered with brilliant Persian flowers, designed by John Fowler. There was red carpet and red lacquered doors – even the closets were lined in red. Red picture frames were filled with photographs of friends and family, both old and new, including the Duke of Windsor in his kilt. Vreeland's favourite deep red peonies often filled the vases. It was chaos but it worked.

What I love about this room is the excess and fun of it all. In a small apartment, high above Park Avenue and the concrete jungle of New York, it cleverly used mirrors and screens to make it seem grander and much larger than it really was.

OPPOSITE – *Detail of the* fleurs du mal *fabric.*
FOLLOWING – *Watercolour interpretation of Diana Vreeland's sitting room.*

CHAPTER 02 – BOTANICALS THROUGH THE AGES

1963
Jacqueline Kennedy: White House Guest Bedroom

*Everything in the White House must have a reason for being there.
It must be restored, and that has nothing to do with decoration.*

– Jacqueline Kennedy

JACQUELINE KENNEDY FAMOUSLY used an orange blossom chintz en masse in one of the smaller guest bedrooms in the White House. She designed the room in collaboration with renowned American designer Rachel Lambert 'Bunny' Mellon, who was also an art collector and advised the Kennedy family on fine arts and antiques during their restoration of the White House. Jacqueline also guided Bunny's redesign of the magnificent White House Rose Garden.

Jacqueline and Bunny used the same chintz textile for a gathered valance, a bedspread, scatter cushions and wall upholstery. The very pretty bedroom was then cleverly anchored with a significant antique bed and furniture placed around the perimeter. They also layered the walls with dark-framed pictures and mirrors, which added contrast. The room became famous and captured the world's imagination, especially in America and the United Kingdom. Once again, a timeless botanical classic was popularised.

OPPOSITE – *Watercolour interpretation of Jacqueline Kennedy's White House guest bedroom.*

CHAPTER 02 — BOTANICALS THROUGH THE AGES

1984
Mario Buatta: Kips Bay Room

There's no date in this room because there's nothing faddish in it. Everything is forever.

– Mario Buatta

AFTER FALLING OUT of fashion after World War II, chintz resurfaced at full speed in the early 1960s. This resurgence was helped by famed American interior designer Mario Buatta and his elaborate, floral-inspired interiors.

In 1984 Buatta – affectionately known as 'The Prince of Chintz' – created one of the most famous Kips Bay Decorator Show House rooms of all time. Furnished with an eclectic collection of antique French and English furniture, it was described by *Architectural Digest* as 'the bedroom that shook the world'. As well as masses of beautiful blue-and-white chintz for curtains and upholstery, Buatta designed a bed that had a white canopy attached to the ceiling and white drapes with bobbin trim.

The room was inspired by the work of Albert Hadley in the 1950s and David Hicks in the 1960s. One of Buatta's design mantras was 'If you're going to do a room where you use the best of the past and the best of today, you have to get it right'. This is the essence of timeless design.

OPPOSITE – *Watercolour interpretation of Mario Buatta's Kips Bay room.*

CHAPTER 02 – BOTANICALS THROUGH THE AGES

INTERVIEW

Sarah MacGregor

HEAD OF DESIGN,
COLEFAX AND FOWLER

How have antique textiles inspired your textile designs over the decades?

Antique textiles are the foundation of the Colefax and Fowler look. Everything we create has its roots in either an antique textile or a genre of historical fabrics or paintings. We are continually adding to it and we're always on the hunt for new pieces that can inspire us. We source historical pieces from all over the world. One of the designs in our new collection is an excellent example of this. 'Fontenoy' was adapted from a 19th-century woven liseré piece. Liseré is a decorative and ornate fabric style that originated in France. The patterns are woven in coloured yarns that contrast with the background, and it often features a border design element. 'Fontenoy' is a beautiful example of a design that has been revisited and reinvented.

Another of our new designs, 'Mariella', was adapted from a beautiful 19th-century printed document. Several of the motifs were repainted and the repeat was adapted but the spirit of the original remains.

Why are botanical and chintz textiles timeless?

Textiles with a botanical inspiration will always play an important part in interior design. They are an easy way to add natural beauty to a space, bringing the feeling of nature into our homes and adding to our sense of wellbeing. They are timeless and can always be adapted with colour and styling to suit any particular moment.

How do you reinvent or update a chintz-inspired interior to prevent it feeling dated?

We always feel that we are doing something of the moment and, of course, we're very interested in the latest trends. We are always looking for ways to keep our collections relevant, whether it's the choice of a certain type of flower or a combination of woven qualities.

What are the most iconic Colefax and Fowler floral or botanical textiles?

'Bowood', 'Fuchsia', 'Snow Tree', 'Summerby' and 'Tree Poppy'.

OPPOSITE – *Colefax and Fowler textiles:* **1.** *Bowood, Grey/Green;* **2.** *Tree Poppy, Red Forrest;* **3.** *Snow Tree,* **4.** *Summerby, Pink; Aqua;* **5.** *Fuschia, Blue/Leaf;* **6.** *Snow Tree, Blue;* **7.** *Bowood, Blue/Grey.*

Designing with Floral Textiles

CHAPTER 03

Borrow from the best of the past, but be clever and reinvent it to create something new.

Designing with Floral Textiles

Throughout history, chintz and botanical-inspired textiles have made frequent appearances on the interior design scene and our love affair with them continues. But how does an idea resurface and become popular time after time? And who decides that it should?

DESIGN IDEAS OFTEN build on the work of other designers – to understand an aesthetic, it is important to consider where it began. The best tip I can give aspiring interior designers is to never stop reading. Read about significant designers from the past and the designers who inspired them. Don't just look at the pictures; immerse yourself in the history of their lives, their inspiration and their principles. Read about architecture, art and the history of furniture. Then you can build on and strengthen the framework of your own aesthetic.

Search out iconic and timeless products and ideas with classic foundations and long histories. Something with a 500-year-old lifespan and a strong narrative will always draw my attention. Borrow from the best of the past, but be clever and reinvent it to create something new.

OPPOSITE – *Working with colour and pattern.*

CHAPTER 03 – DESIGNING WITH FLORAL TEXTILES

How to Make an Ordinary Room Sing

STEP 1

SELECT A VIBRANT HERO

The sadder the space, the louder your hero can be. I encourage you to choose something whimsical, with movement and that is full of colour. If you are brave and use it on large surfaces, like walls, even better!

STEP 2

ADD STRUCTURE

You will need to balance your hero out with some structure, for example, geometric or lineal forms or block colours. Natural textures can also provide a lovely contrast to bold colours. If you have used your hero on a large surface, try to apply your structured element on an equally prominent surface, like the floor or several large pieces of furniture.

STEP 3

BALANCE THE ROOM

When you have selected the major design elements, stop and look at what the room needs. Even in a bold room, all the elements should be complementary. Nothing should stand out as being garish. Does your room need some white? Could it do with some natural textures? Artworks in a contrasting style or colour can also work.

OPPOSITE – *A very ordinary room in the Coote & Co. studio was transformed in a fabulous bedroom using Soane Britain's 'Palampore Blossom' wallpaper in pink and red.*

TIP

If your budget does not allow for an elaborate wall covering, try a beautiful dark paint colour. Layer artwork or large pieces of antique floral textiles over the wall, almost like a tapestry. Making the walls darker will create a cosy and layered room.

Try a beautiful four-poster bed (I custom designed and manufactured this one, but you can pick these up at auction) that literally fills the room. The smaller the room, the more you should fill it. The opposite applies to a large room: the larger it is, the emptier you should leave it.

CHAPTER 03 – DESIGNING WITH FLORAL TEXTILES

Designing with Botanical Textiles

When you are creating a textile scheme, including a botanical print can add movement and story to the space. You can do this on a large, medium or small scale.

LARGE – Choose a large, loud and colourful botanical print and plaster the walls with it. It should really dominate the space and define the room. Be brave. Throw all the rules out the window and own it.

MEDIUM – Use a botanical print on a sofa or a pair of large armchairs. Integrate and balance this with other textiles to provide some relief.

SMALL – Select a floral textile and use it sparingly, for example on a small scatter cushion or a lampshade. Gather the fabric on the lampshade to obscure the pattern if the prettiness of the textile is too challenging.

OPPOSITE – *I went large for my clients in this coastal bedroom using Soane Britain's 'Dianthus Chintz – Lapis' to adorn the walls. Using it en masse creates a joyful environment and the white background ensures the busy pattern still feels elegant.*

ABOVE – *The motif on the Namay Samay 'Alya-Chota' textile used on this bedhead was inspired by a 19th-century Persian print. Pairing it with textured wallpaper, bold green picture frames and geometric lampshades creates a harmonious space.*

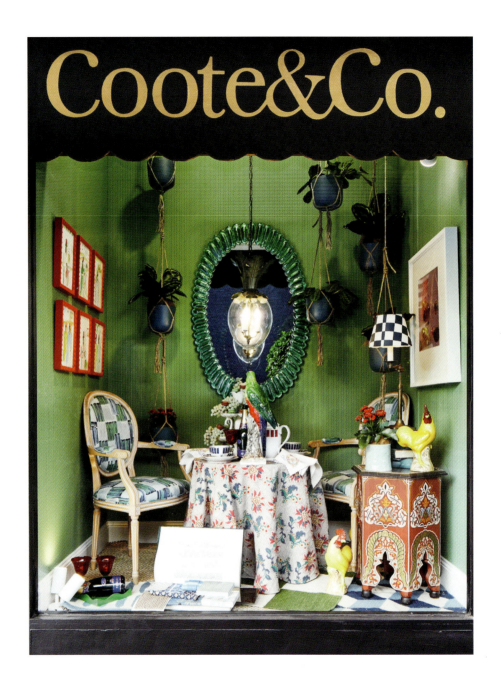

TIP

Throw in an ugly duckling to prevent a room becoming too pretty or perfect. It can be fun to add a random, unusual or humorous print or artwork to shake things up and balance out prettiness. I currently have an ugly but charming beaded porcupine on a side table in my sitting room. A friend brought it back from her African travels. It's random, but it's handmade and has tons of character and personality.

CHAPTER 03 – DESIGNING WITH FLORAL TEXTILES

How to Use Botanical Prints in a Contemporary Setting

STEP 1

SELECT A FLORAL TEXTILE

Think outside the square. Rather than running to your favourite textile house, consider antique textiles. I love walking into a room and seeing a textile I don't know. Antique textiles immediately add authenticity, interest and charm. They can also be a cost-effective and sustainable way to repurpose something that would otherwise have been discarded.

STEP 2

ADD STRUCTURE

Include lineal textiles like different scaled checks, stripes or plaids to balance, support and anchor large and smaller designs. Remember that opposites attract. Curved shapes sit well next to straight ones. Put chaos next to crisp, hard next to soft and masculine next to feminine. Robert Kime once said, 'Put something modest next to something quite grand. They will help each other to be more interesting.'

STEP 3

MODERNISE THE LOOK

Move away from the excess of the 1980s. Be inspired by the best parts of your memories of your grandmother's home, rather than rolling it out in full. Reinvent botanical-inspired schemes and curate relevant contemporary themes that breathe life into an interior. Use modern materials like Perspex, glass or lacquer next to chintz or botanical textiles to modernise them. Put something old-fashioned next to something edgy or unusual. Modernise and layer the look even more using contemporary pieces of furniture, lighting and artwork.

OPPOSITE – *The prettiness of this 'Dianthus Chintz Lapis' wallpaper from Soane Britain is balanced by the dark blue linen bedhead, which I intentionally kept simple and contemporary. The pops of green provide a welcome contrast and ensure the room doesn't look flat.*

CHAPTER 03 – DESIGNING WITH FLORAL TEXTILES

STEP 4

CONSIDER SCALE AND TEXTURE

Include a diverse range and scale of textiles – a small ocelot print works well next to a medium-scale check. Consider juxtaposing hard and contrasting textures with soft textiles. You might place a velvet sofa with linen scatter cushions next to a travertine coffee table.

Mixing large-scale textiles with small-scale textiles works. However, combining medium-scale textiles with small-scale textiles usually doesn't. Sometimes two medium-scale patterns can work if the colours are reversed. For example, one medium-scale textile that is predominantly dark blue with a hint of white could work with another that is predominantly white with a small amount of dark green.

It's always a good idea to include a plain coloured or textured textile in the mix to help neutralise things.

Trust your instinct. Understand and learn the building blocks you can use to create a scheme, then establish rules of your own.

ABOVE – The pattern on Lewis & Wood's 'Oxus' mid-scale print is repeated many times across the bedhead. The textile is balanced with textured chevron cushions, a contemporary gloss bedside table and a striped lampshade.

OPPOSITE – Schumacher's 'Sinhala Sidewall' wallpaper is a large-scale print, which was perfect for getting a rambling effect of the vines on the walls. Because this pattern has so much movement, I grounded it with a cobalt blue bedhead, small-scale geometric cushions and dark oak bedside tables.

CHAPTER 03 – DESIGNING WITH FLORAL TEXTILES

STEP 5

CONSIDER COLOUR AND QUANTITIES

Note the colours of your main hero botanical print. They will inspire the colour palette for your entire textile scheme. This doesn't mean you need to match those colours identically. For example, slightly clashing colours can be very interesting to the eye.

If you lose your nerve and only want a pop of a textile or colour, use it on a scatter cushion or occasional chair, rather than an entire sofa. Similarly, if you are mad about a textile but can't afford lots of it, use it on a cushion rather than an entire sofa.

Think carefully about where you plan to use each textile and how much of it you want to see in the room. Looking at 20-centimetre-square samples of a textile is not the same as looking at it en masse.

OPPOSITE, ABOVE AND FOLLOWING – *Clashing, complementary and tonal. All three rooms use colour and pattern in different ways.*

CHAPTER 03 – DESIGNING WITH FLORAL TEXTILES

CASE STUDY

Coote & Co.: Office Bedroom

It is far easier to create an interesting interior from a space when it has good bones to start with. It might have high ceilings or gorgeous natural light. It might possess interesting architectural details or beautiful panelled walls. But what do you do when a room has absolutely nothing going for it? How do you transform an ugly duckling into something interesting, timeless and comfortable?

WE HAD THIS exact challenge with the studio bedroom at Coote & Co. It was a dark, run-down, south-facing room with one tiny broken window. It had low ceilings, strip lighting and decrepit old floorboards. It reminded me of a jail cell. The footprint was small – roughly 3 x 4 metres. However, I felt that with some clever selections it could become a cosy bedroom and an inviting space.

We chose a Soane Britain wallpaper called 'Palampore Blossom' in a pink and red colourway. The large-scale, botanical print was bursting with colour and we knew it would provide the room with focus, depth and character.

The paper was inspired by an 18th-century Indian palampore. A palampore is a hand-painted bedcover that was often produced for European colonists. Each one could take hours to create. They usually had a series of complex or elaborate patterns that showed off a wide variety of plants, flowers and animals. The wallpaper immediately lifted the room from glum to glam.

OPPOSITE AND FOLLOWING – *Once the renovation was completed, our formerly drab office bedroom was unrecognisable; it became vibrant, layered and beautiful. The all-white bed is a prominent feature and ensures that the colours and patterns are not overwhelming.*

CHAPTER 03 – DESIGNING WITH FLORAL TEXTILES

The next-largest surface area was the floor. The bold wallpaper needed relief and the opposite of something whimsical and unruly is something structured.

I once stayed in an Italian bedroom that had large-scale green-and-white chequerboard tiles on the floor. It was fabulous and unusual. I wondered if I could reproduce that look in a flat weave rug, layered over sisal. It could add the structure the space needed.

My friend, the late interior designer Stuart Rattle, once told me that to create a new interior product you must commit to producing it three or four times before you could perfect it. He said it was a process that could take up to three years.

I often use my own interior spaces as the testing ground for new ideas. I was trained to create unusual and one-off interior furniture, textiles and lighting and this remains one of my greatest passions. It can take time, but when a creation works, it is enormously satisfying. It also adds a sense of authenticity and a unique quality to an interior. The knowledge that no one else has that same piece is thrilling to me.

We successfully produced the rug with a talented Indian rug maker, Kamal Ahmad Ansari. We used New Zealand wool and selected an appropriate scale and colour. Then we put the rug through an aging process to make it look as if it had been faded by the sun over time. The final outcome provided the room with relief from the pink and red botanical walls.

The final step with this room was to balance its strength. The pink, red and green were very strong, so the bedhead, mirror and ottoman were kept textural and fresh in off-white to provide light relief.

Small-scale textiles in muted and earthy tones completed the balancing act. We introduced these through scatter cushions on the bed and beautiful hand-painted lampshades made by hand in London by my friend Alvaro Picardo.

An oak chest of drawers from Graham Geddes Antiques helped to anchor the colour within the room. The hand-painted hardwood Gustavian bedside tables that I had designed and created in Ireland twenty years ago also gave a pop of fresh white and timber. Another first-time creation was the mirror, which I designed in resin and had a bevelled edge and antique mirror. The mirror was a one-off – it is unique. My husband, Geordie, says it reminds him of teeth. This was not my intention, but it makes me laugh and adds character and humour to the space.

Finally, we hung three prints, including a small Lucy Boyd landscape painted on timber, which was a gift from my husband. They were like windows into another world. The final room is simple and unpretentious, yet fresh and functional.

ABOVE AND OPPOSITE – *Brass, timber, white linens, contemporary artworks and a bold rug come together to create harmony in this space.*

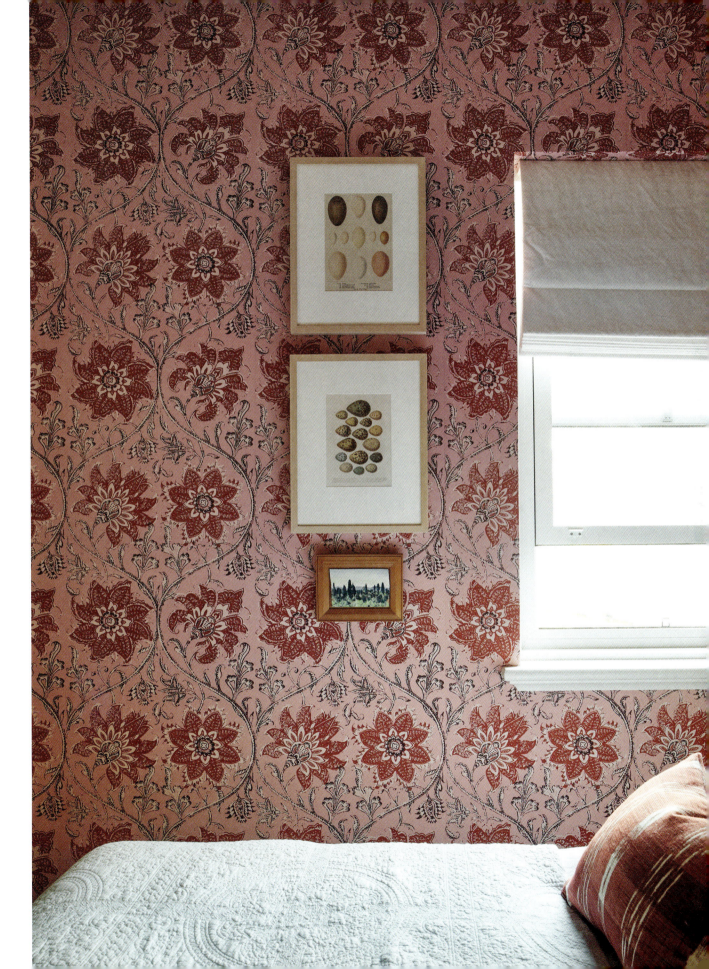

CHAPTER 03 – DESIGNING WITH FLORAL TEXTILES

CASE STUDY

Sophisticated Home Office

This home-office space had little room for upholstery or textiles, so the impact of the design really needed to come from the walls and vertical surfaces. The rest of the house was quite contemporary, with strong mid-century modern furnishings. We wanted to ensure this room made sense with the rest of the house, while also giving it some decorative, feminine elements.

THE FIRST THING we selected was 'McGegan Rose' wallpaper by Timorous Beasties. Its clean lines and simple three-tone palette make it a contemporary take on floral design and, although the black and white is bold and dark, the rambling roses are a romantic touch. This room didn't get a lot of natural light, so the dark wallpaper really worked. Because 'McGegan Rose' is quite decorative, we created all the other elements with simplicity and modernity in mind.

We designed built-in cupboards to provide office storage and space for wardrobe overflow from the master bedroom. The cupboards are a significant design element – they are more than 3 metres high and flank the fireplace along one whole wall. They had to stand up to the strength of the wallpaper and also provide a contrast to its darkness. We chose Resene Gordons Green paint and used it in high-gloss two-pack on the cupboard doors, which had no profile detailing at all. Even though this is a dark colour, the gloss reflects light and makes it appear brighter. The large swathes of plain gloss contrasted beautifully with the light-absorbing wallpaper and provided a colour element to the design.

As the major wall elements in this room were bold and dark, we had to make sure that the furniture didn't feel heavy. We selected a beautiful desk with slender, turned-wood legs and a glass top that seemed to float on its supports. The form was light, but the design was sophisticated and it worked well as the centrepiece of the room.

We also wanted to bring in some more natural elements to the space to further contrast the gloss and matt. A chunky, woven abaca rug grounded the space and the weave of the rug provided a subtle linear element to the design.

OPPOSITE – *Timorous Beasties' 'McGegan Rose' wallpaper is undoubtedly the hero of this room. The clean, contemporary look and textures of the gloss green joinery and the sisal rug balance out its busyness.*

CHAPTER 03 – DESIGNING WITH FLORAL TEXTILES

Finally, the room needed a small injection of colour. Vibrant coral velvet on the footstools and a similar tone on the desk chair gave the palette the lift it needed without being overbearing.

We hung six black-and-white photographs that the client had taken on their travels. Not only were the images striking on their own, but the scale and repetition added a structured layer to the whimsical walls. These pictures were reflected in the mantle-to-ceiling mirror above the fireplace, which also helped to bounce light around the room. The lamp and sculpture provided a simple, yet sophisticated, brass element to the room, completing the balancing act.

The completed room feels bold, modern and feminine. Although it's not the first thing that strikes you, it has all the elements of an indoor garden – florals, greenery, natural materials and a pop of perfect coral.

ABOVE AND OPPOSITE – *An Italian-made desk floats elegantly in this space, and the black-and-white photography and interesting brass accessories provide the finishing touches.*

Antique Textiles

CHAPTER 04

Innovation is often the ability to reach into the past and bring back what is good, what is beautiful, what is useful, what is lasting.

– *Sister Parish*

Antique Textiles

I dislike waste. I love being resourceful. It is easy to create an interior from items that are sparkling and new – anyone can do that. I prefer to use antique furniture and textiles in my interiors.

UNTIL THE 1850S, when the first synthetic dyes were produced, the only way to colour fabrics was with natural dyes made from roots, flowers, leaves and berries. You still can't go wrong with the colours of plants and flowers and the cycles of nature. Think of the hues of ripe blackberries, sunny marigolds and multicoloured onion skins – do you see where I'm going with this?

The pigments of antique textiles are unusual and impossible to replicate using modern machines or synthetic dyes. The effect of light on the patina and texture over time is authentic and often exquisite. I like reinventing something to give it a new purpose. I love reusing beautiful handmade pieces and saving them from becoming landfill.

A designer outfit becomes outdated within months. There's always a new fashion that is loudly proclaimed to be the latest trend, but it never lasts long. The interior industry can be guilty of this as well. Too often, people look at the white boucle sofa they bought last year and decide it is dated. Off to the tip it goes, only to be replaced with a trendy, new, mid-century-inspired sofa that has been mass-produced overseas.

Both the fashion and interior industries need to reduce their contributions to landfill. In *The Sound of Music*, Maria had the right idea when she sewed new clothes for the Von Trapp children from old curtains. We all need to look at how we can reuse, reinvent or, better still, buy once and buy well.

OPPOSITE – For this country home, we salvaged silk curtains from the client's grandmother's house and used them to create scatter cushions featuring peacocks and flowers. It provided a wonderful sense of history and shared memory.

FOLLOWING RIGHT – Wendy Lewis from The Textile Trunk: 'This textile was part of a large bed set that was sadly burnt in a house fire in 2017. This was one of the only scraps that survived. This amazing fabric was hand-block printed in Mulhouse, France, and dates back to the late 18th century.'

TIP

If you are updating your interior, consider salvaging relatively new or good-quality textiles from your old furniture, scatter cushions or bedheads. You could have them dry-cleaned and reimagined as something else, gift them to a friend or donate to an op shop. One man's trash is another man's treasure.

Get creative! Use old curtains as a runner or tablecloth for your dining room table or turn them into napkins. They are the perfect thickness. You could also repurpose them as a unique bedspread or use them to reupholster an occasional chair or ottoman.

Dress your home with handmade fabrics created by global artisans using traditional techniques – North African Berber textiles in the colours of nature and Indian teal linens are just two examples.

THIS SPREAD — *1. Soane Britain, Pineapple Silhouette, Ochre on Stone Linen; 2. Soane Britain, Sargent Stripe, Old Gold; 3. Rose Tarlow, Country Cloth, Penny/Natural; 4. Soane Britain, Date, Gold; 5. Boon & Up, Langtaa; 6. International Floor Coverings, Manzanilla 2 Tone (Pearl-Malay) Abaca; 7. Soane Britain, Persian Maze, Ochre; 8. Soane Britain, Corded Stripe, Red; 9. Bennison Fabrics, Dragon Flower, Pink Green on Oyster*

THIS SPREAD — *1. Antique textile; 2. Namay Samay, Hilsa, Madder; 3. Tango White Marble; 4. Schumacher Zonda, Indigo; 5. Pierre Frey, Angkor, Emeraude; 6. Soane Britain, Seaweed Lace, Emerald on Stone Linen*

THIS SPREAD — *1. Antique textile; 2. Namay Samay, Hilsa, Frangipani; 3. Moroccan tile in Blush; 4. Namay Samay, Sitaron, Rose*

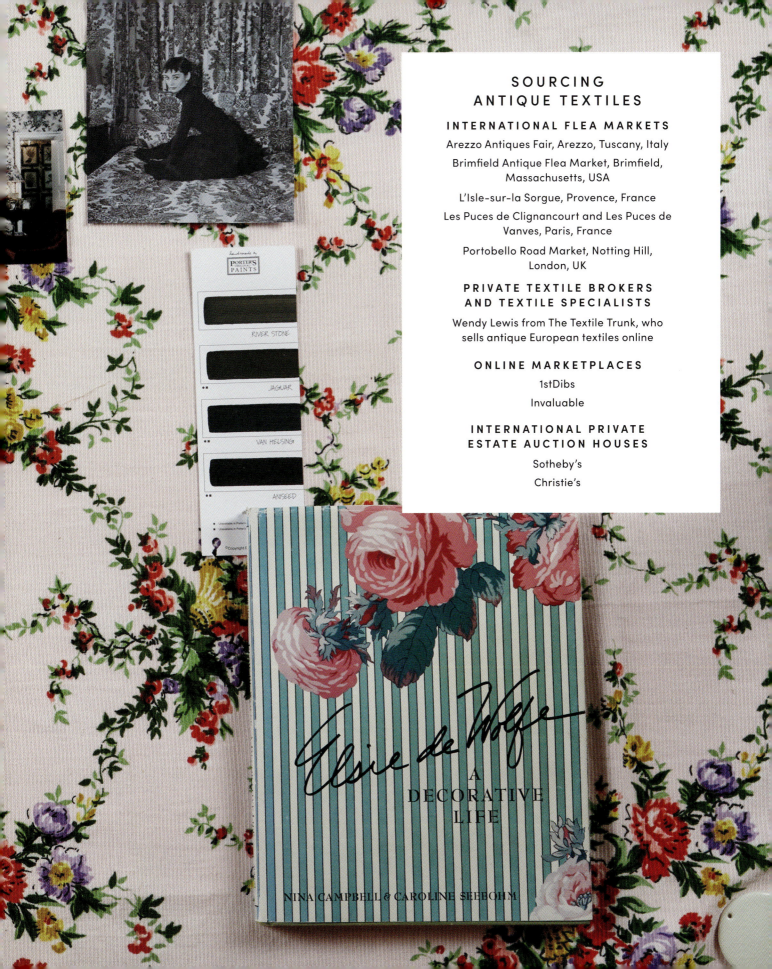

SOURCING ANTIQUE TEXTILES

INTERNATIONAL FLEA MARKETS

Arezzo Antiques Fair, Arezzo, Tuscany, Italy

Brimfield Antique Flea Market, Brimfield, Massachusetts, USA

L'Isle-sur-la Sorgue, Provence, France

Les Puces de Clignancourt and Les Puces de Vanves, Paris, France

Portobello Road Market, Notting Hill, London, UK

PRIVATE TEXTILE BROKERS AND TEXTILE SPECIALISTS

Wendy Lewis from The Textile Trunk, who sells antique European textiles online

ONLINE MARKETPLACES

1stDibs

Invaluable

INTERNATIONAL PRIVATE ESTATE AUCTION HOUSES

Sotheby's

Christie's

CHAPTER 04 – ANTIQUE TEXTILES

INTERVIEW

Alexandra Tolstoy

CURATOR, THE TOLSTOY EDIT

What do you love about antique textiles and how do you use them in your interior?

I love the designs, colours and textures. Because they were always handmade, they have charming inconsistencies and feel so personal. Although they often met a practical need, I love the idea that beauty was always seen as a necessity. The colours are from natural dyes and are easier and more harmonious on the eye than chemical dyes, and work juxtaposed with anything – it's the same for natural fibres. It always amazes me how rarely something modern can be as good as something old!

Where do you like to find or buy antique textiles?

I make regular trips to Kyrgyzstan to source the Central Asian textiles for my business, but I started buying in 1999 when I rode the Silk Road and we stopped in Bukhara and Samarkand [in Uzbekistan]. For English textiles, there is a wonderfully eccentric antiques dealer near my cottage who always has lots of gems.

Why do you use botanical, chintz and floral textiles in your interiors?

Nature is a huge part of my life – I couldn't live without my riding trips to Kyrgyzstan – so it's a natural extension that I love floral chintzes. At my cottage, my children and I live as much outside as inside. I like to feel there's not a huge division between them.

How do you mix, modernise or update an interior using floral textiles?

I like mixing textiles and don't have rules but I do find it helps to have a common colour. In my cottage office, I wanted something very English to ground it – everything else in the room is Russian or Central Asian – so I chose the classic Colefax and Fowler 'Fuchsia' chintz. Red and green also run through the room so it's in tune.

What drew you to the antique Russian textile you reimagined? What do you know about its history?

I first discovered it in Uzbekistan. A wonderful woman called Susan Meller has collected incredible cottons made by the Russians for the Central Asian market before the 1917 Revolution. They are extraordinarily modern and huge feats of design. It was very difficult to choose one to re-create but I looked at my cottage's colours and this was the one I thought would work best in an English home. Love Your Home printed it in a lovely crisp cotton fabric.

OPPOSITE – *The pattern on the Alexandra Armchair was inspired by Alexandra Tolstoy's collection of antique textiles and her passion for mixing and matching them.*

Using Colours From Nature

CHAPTER 05

When you are searching for the perfect colour to paint a house, look at the trunks of significant local trees. There will aways be a trio of colours to tap into.

– John Coote

OPPOSITE – *Standing outside, you can easily see how the garden has inspired this green and white sunroom. I also love how the beautifully aged pink of the house's exterior contrasts the vibrant green within.*

ABOVE – *Close up you can see several different shades of neutrals, browns and greens – a colour palette just waiting to be explored.*

Using Colours From Nature

Greens

THE SECRET TO using greens in interiors is to look at the shades of green outside your window or in your favourite green space. If it's a lush landscape – somewhere sub-tropical, for instance – you'll see more colours than you can count. When I created my kitchen at Marnanie, the predominant greens outside were in the rhododendrons, *Dicksonia* tree ferns, laurel trees and hydrangeas. I picked leaves from them all and literally laid them down on the ground with a large selection of green paint samples. The paint colour that looked like another layer of green within all those leaf colours was the one I chose for the joinery. The idea is to use different shades of the colours from nature to replicate the layering you see outside.

OPPOSITE – *Earthy greens and browns in this country home's powder room create a warm and interesting space. The Barneby Gates 'Pheasant' wallpaper is a playful nod to the countryside, and the handmade Moroccan floor tiles have a lovely, aged look. The lacquer mirror and ochre marble vanity elevate the space.*

THIS SPREAD — **1.** *Diane Bergeron, Park Avenue Petite, Moss;* **2.** *Antique Textile, USA;* **3.** *Namay Samay, Hilsa, Pine;* **4.** *Barneby Gates, Pheasant, Camo Green;* **5.** *Phillip Jeffries, Juicy Jute II, Racing Green;* **6.** *Namay Samay, Zeimoto, Conifero;* **7.** *Warwick, Cleo, Forest;* **8.** *Artedomus, Smeraldo, Honed;* **9.** *Manuel Canovas, Rimini, Olive;* **10.** *Manuel Canovas, Rivoli, Prairie;* **11.** *Woodcut, European Oak, Thistle*

OPPOSITE AND ABOVE — *The green wool upholstered walls are the hero of this hearty dining room. The wonderful sense of cocooning is brightened by the raspberry ribbon framing the room and the high glossy ceiling.*

ABOVE AND OPPOSITE – *The bar is connected to the green dining room. The colour of the dining room ceiling is used here on the joinery, but in a lower level of gloss.*

THIS SPREAD – **1.** Pierre Frey, Le Paravent, Chinois; **2.** Manuel Canovas, Apolline, Prairie; **3.** Artedomus, Quaresto, Honed; **4.** Antique Textile, B&G, 05212; **5.** Schumacher, Edwin Stripe Wide, Leaf; **6.** Colefax and Fowler, Mecox, Fern; **7.** Dogwood Fabrics, 9110-34, Olive; **8.** Colefax and Fowler, Wide Picot Braid, Mid Green; **9.** Bennison Fabrics, Cinnabar, Green Blue on Oyster Linen; **10.** GP & J Baker, Ikat Bokhara, Emerald

PREVIOUS SPREAD AND OPPOSITE – *'Calm Green' by Resene Paints was selected for this kitchen. The fresh white marble bench tops and brass accents pair beautifully with the joinery.*

ABOVE – *Green on green with neutrals in-between.*

ABOVE – *Fresh green and white details.*

OPPOSITE – *The key to making a single colour work en masse is to integrate different textures and tones. In my bedroom at Marnanie, the green Murano glass mirror pops off the texture of the wallpaper.*

CHAPTER 05 — USING COLOURS FROM NATURE

Blues

SIT AND LOOK CAREFULLY at the colour blue in nature, especially in the ocean, rivers, lakes and other waterways. You'll see hundreds of blue hues in the landscape, the flora and even the fauna. Forget the boring cliché of the beach house in blue and white. Choosing many shades of blue and using them cleverly creates a clean and crisp interior with subtle layers that mimic nature's palette.

OPPOSITE – The library at Marnanie features a glorious mix of clashing patterns and tonal blues.
ABOVE – This William Yeoward textile has all the blues of the ocean – perfect for this waterfront residence.

THIS SPREAD – **1.** Colefax and Fowler, Levan, Navy; **2.** Soane Britain, Dianthus Chintz, Lapis; **3.** Pierre Frey, Angkor, Atlantique; **4.** Colefax and Fowler, Yatton Stripe, Navy; **5.** Colefax and Fowler, Panthera, Navy; **6.** Colefax and Fowler, Wide Picot Braid, Red; **7.** Antique Textile; **8.** Soane Britain, Wilton Vine, Azure; **9.** Artedomus, Quaresto, Honed; **10.** Colefax and Fowler, Mecox, Fern; **11.** GP & J Baker, Ikat Bokhara, Emerald; **12.** Antique Textile, B&G, 05212; **13.** The Marble House, Arabescato Vagli; **14.** Bennison Fabrics, Cinnabar, Green Blue on Oyster Linen; **15.** Pierre Frey, Le Paravent, Chinois; **16.** Manuel Canovas, Apolline, Prairie; **17.** Inchyra, Dianthus; **18.** Colefax and Folwer, Mecox, Blue; **19.** Colefax and Fowler, Sackville, Blue; **20.** Soane Britain, Etched Pineapple, Cream on Jasper Blue

OPPOSITE, ABOVE AND FOLLOWING —
Farrow & Ball's striped wallpaper creates a sophisticated, inviting backdrop on which the other colours and patterns can play.

THIS SPREAD — **1.** *Soane Britain, Coromandel Tulip, Walnut and Neel;* **2.** *Sibyl Colefax & John Fowler, Fleurette;* **3.** *George Spencer Designs, Herringbone Stripe, Cinnamon;* **4.** *Dedar Milano, Adamo & Eva, ADAMO-116;* **5.** *Lewis & Wood, Speedwell, Wedgewood Blue;* **6.** *Stroheim, Mariposa Marine;* **7.** *Sibyl Colefax & John Fowler, Teal Seaweed;* **8.** *Travertine, honed and unfilled;* **9.** *Antique textile*

OPPOSITE AND ABOVE —
Blue, yellow and white – the quintessential beachside colour palette.

ABOVE AND OPPOSITE – *Classic blue and white stripes are balanced with greens and neutrals.*
FOLLOWING – *The linear blue elements in this room work together because they vary in scale and tone.*

OPPOSITE, ABOVE AND FOLLOWING —
Elevated design is all in the details. Large, glossy, custom-made trays provide the contemporary pop this living room needed. The brass rods on the Roger Oates stair runner are the finishing touch on this look.

THIS SPREAD — **1.** *GP & J Baker, Thornham, Spice;* **2.** *Samuel & Sons, Sloane Velvet Border, Russet;* **3.** *Antique Textile;* **4.** *Schumacher, Garden Gate Chintz, Magenta;* **5.** *Bennison Fabrics, Hollyhock, Blue on Oyster Linen;* **6.** *Soane Britain, Persian Maze, Lacquer Red;* **7.** *The Marble House, Rosa Aurora Marble;* **8.** *Pierre Frey, Fadini, Caprirosa;* **9.** *Schumacher, Zoe Linen Ruche, Blanc;* **10.** *Brunschwig & Fils, Chamas Stripe, Tomato;* **11.** *GP & J Baker, Ikat Bokhara, Neutral;* **12.** *Susan Deliss, Mini Weave, Red/Cream;* **13.** *Woodcut, European Oak, Pearl White;* **14.** *Elliott Clarke Textiles, Millbrook, Cherry;* **15.** *Colefax and Fowler, Arlington Bullion Fringe, Pink/Green;* **16.** *Soane Britain, Jasmine and Frangipani, Original*

CHAPTER 05 – USING COLOURS FROM NATURE

Pinks and Reds

PINKS AND REDS are the drama queens of nature. A rose garden in bloom with a mass of pink and red roses is a gift to the senses. As I look out from my tiny pink dining room, I can see a brilliant pink fuchsia sitting next to a mollis azalea and a pale pink rhododendron – the colours both clash wonderfully and work harmoniously.

If I had just painted the walls in a glamorous pink and left it at that, it would have looked too intense. The important thing is to keep going until you achieve the balance you see in nature. Keep layering your jewel tones and remember to give the design some relief – for example, a green tablecloth and vases.

ABOVE – This pink dining room is definitely the 'drama queen' of my home. Many a raucous dinner party has been held here. You can only feel happy in a space this vibrant.

THIS SPREAD — *1. Howe at 36 Bourne Street, Ripstop, Ruby;
2. Namay Samay, Sharang Tara, Indigo; 3. Bennison Fabrics,
Onikoko, Reds on Beige Linen; 4. Namay Samay, Kadva, Mughal;
5. Jean Monro, Soapberry, Rosehip; 6. Antique Textile, B&G, 05210;
7. George Feathers, Fumed Arctic Brushed and Oiled;
8. Dogwood Fabrics, 9112-54, Geranium;
9. Namay Samay, Sitaron, Scarlet*

Introducing Natural Textures

CHAPTER 06

The poetry of the Earth is never dead.

– John Keats

Introducing Natural Textures

I love using natural textures because they bring the outside world in – not just visually, but texturally. Sisal, grass cloth, wicker and cane are some of my favourites and they're also pleasingly inexpensive. Sisal is a very strong natural fibre that was used by the Aztecs to make rope – I like to use it as a floor covering but you can achieve the same feeling with grass cloth wallpaper, natural cane furniture or even small touches, like wicker placemats. When you touch these rough natural textures, you are reminded of the feeling of grass under your bare feet or the bark of a tree.

OPPOSITE – *The hearty texture of the exquisite timber and stone inlay flooring, layered with sisal rugs, grounds the vibrancy of this green-and-white sunroom.*

FOLLOWING – *This bedroom is all about texture. The camel grasscloth that envelops the room is reminiscent of fine paperbark. Navy velvet adds softness and a sense of luxury.*

PREVIOUS AND OPPOSITE – *Stone, timber, lacquer, ceramic, linen, silk, sisal, bronze and brass. Layers of varied materials make for a successful space.*

ABOVE – *A collection of nature's textures – a feast for the eyes.*

OPPOSITE AND ABOVE — *Smooth leather sits against natural grasscloth walls and a silk-fringed sofa brushes against a wool plaid rug. Opposite textures work together in the best way.*

FOLLOWING — *This light-filled entrance is kept simple with timber, abaca, bronze lighting and a smart wool stair runner.*

OPPOSITE AND ABOVE – *The use of colour was pared right back in this beach house. Texture is the quiet hero of every space.*

FOLLOWING – *The inspiration from this room was plucked straight from the ocean. Layers of blue are complemented with honed travertine that echoes the movement of sand, sunny pops of ochre and the natural warmth of timber.*

TIP

Nature's textural scheme is often where the magic lies. Every beach has its own local stone and local shrubs and features specific types and colours of sand, shells and moss. The water is a unique shade somewhere between green and blue. The hues in the sky are constantly changing, from dawn to dusk and with the incoming weather.

Working with Flowers and Greenery

CHAPTER 07

No greater confidence can be offered than the timelessness and elegance of the outside world.

Working with Flowers and Greenery

As a designer, working with flowers and greenery is not dissimilar to the way that chefs work with ingredients. To achieve the best results, they choose ingredients that are seasonal and, preferably, local. If you have the luxury of access to a garden (or a friend's garden), whether it's a small yard, a large garden or a rural block, that's great. If not, you can still use these ideas with purchased flowers and greenery.

I am extremely fortunate to live on a large country property. The beauty of the passing seasons constantly inspires me with new ways to embellish my interiors. When we first moved to Marnanie, I no longer needed to buy flowers from a market or shop. They can be higher maintenance and you may have to boil the stems to make them look good, but I love using what's available in my own backyard. It's also great for the environment, because it doesn't involve shipping blooms from the other side of the world. And it's much kinder on your wallet – another big win.

At Marnanie, we're incredibly spoiled in spring, with its abundance of vibrant colour. Summer brings the blooming of the herbaceous border, which provides a variegated carpet of green, white and purple foliage. A different colour palette emerges in autumn – beautiful, earthy colours and deeper shades of red, burgundy and orange signal a last farewell to summer. Even in the middle of winter, I can bring snowdrops and hellebores inside – winter blooms are harder to get and therefore more precious. You use what's available or do without.

PREVIOUS AND OPPOSITE – *Foraging in my garden is one of my favourite pastimes. I love cutting large branches of beech or masses of hydrangea to style in my home.*

CHAPTER 07 – WORKING WITH FLOWERS AND GREENERY

FIG.1

FIG.2

FIG.3

FIG.4

FIG.5

Once you've assembled your blooms and greenery, it's time to pick the right vase. A great collection of vases is a must-have, not a nice-to-have. I love collecting large-scale vases – they suit my house. Experience has taught me they can be hard to find online or in shops, so I keep an eye out for them at auctions and snap them up straight away.

When I'm working with flowers and greenery, I like tapping into the existing colours within a room. For example, if I'm working in a blue room, I use blooms in white or blue or even yellow, which can be wonderful. In my pink dining room, flowers in clashing shades of pinks and bold reds really enhance the space.

ABOVE – *Hydrangeas (Fig. 1), dogwoods (Fig. 2), peonies (Fig. 3), lilies of the valley (Fig. 4) and Japanese anemones (Fig. 5) are some of my favourite flowers.*

OPPOSITE – *Our mischievous labrador Bobby keeps me company in the garden.*

TIP

My favourite branches to use inside are beech in spring and maple in autumn. Arrange three large branches for drama and impact. It's all about the vase height – aim to have the greenery well above the top of the vase. Keep the water topped up – try to always have the vase four-fifths full. The branches will last for up to a month if you keep the water fresh.

TIP

Keep it simple. Arrange one thing from the garden en masse in a vase. Keep the leaves above the top of the vase – rotting leaves produce bacteria and turn the water bad.

Planting tulips always reminds me of Mother's Day. Keep the bulbs in the freezer until you need them. Plant them in two layers in the pot for fullness.

CHAPTER 07 – WORKING WITH FLOWERS AND GREENERY

The Bulb Lawn

Marnanie's former owners, Kevin O'Neill and his partner, John Graham, used to plant unsold bulbs from Kevin's shop in the lawn. Geordie and I have recently done the same with leftover bulbs from Riddell's Creek Nursery. The bulbs bloom for months: first come the snowdrops, then crocuses, daffodils, hyacinths, primroses, bluebells, tulips and – my absolute favourite – lilies of the valley. It is a riot of colours and scents and provides endless options for our vases.

OPPOSITE AND ABOVE – *The bulb lawn in spring.*
FOLLOWING – *Looking down over the bulb lawn and the herbaceous border.*

CHAPTER 07 – WORKING WITH FLOWERS AND GREENERY

Creating a Flower Room

Traditionally, a flower room is a practical and charming space set aside in a large country house for cutting and storing flowers. A little slice of outdoorsy paradise, it would usually be filled with muddy boots and jackets, sturdy tables and shelves for storage, and buckets and jugs overflowing with blooms.

YET IT IS much more than that. It is part of the interior, but it sets the stage for the joys outdoors. An in-between space imbued with a certain magical charm, it often contains the fresh, sweet fragrances of the outside world. It showcases the bounty of nature, but it is not staged or designed to impress. The space is entirely personal. And the more stories it holds, the better.

Today, the concept of the flower room has undergone a transformation. It is being reinvented and redefined in spaces of all shapes and sizes. Whether you have a small pad in the city or a large home in the countryside, a flower room is within your reach.

When I was creating my own flower room, I was influenced by the inspiring interpretations of designers like American designer Charlotte Moss; senior design director at Sybil Colefax and John Fowler, Emma Burns; New York-based architect GP Schafer (one of the greats) and, of course, garden designer Charlie McCormick. I also love the Land Gardeners, Bridget Elworthy and Henrietta Courtauld, and their ideas on creating a cutting garden.

As a nature-inspired response to design, the primary purpose of a flower room is to create happiness. However, it should also provide suitable storage and be visually appealing. Function and form are equal. And it shouldn't matter how large or small the space (or the budget!). Even if you are renting the smallest apartment, these ideas could inspire your own vision of a flower room to blossom.

CHAPTER 07 – WORKING WITH FLOWERS AND GREENERY

INTERVIEW

Paul Bangay

**FOUNDER & CREATIVE DIRECTOR,
PAUL BANGAY GARDEN DESIGN**

How did your early days designing and working in the garden at Marnanie inform the way you connect your interiors to your own garden?

I first visited Marnanie as a guest of Kevin O'Neill about forty years ago, when I was a very young and naive student. I had never been exposed to such a unique and rarefied world of gardens, interiors and design. After passing through the heavy wrought-iron gates at the end of the long, steep gravel drive, I entered a dreamlike woodland of towering sequoias underplanted with flowering bulbs and carpets of ferns. The house was dark and dramatic and full of wonderful treasures, with sumptuous bowls of flowers everywhere. It was my first flush of inspiration – I knew this space was going to influence me for the rest of my life. Ever since that first visit I have clung on to that feeling of deep inspiration and joy. Woodland plantings are still my favourite moments in gardens. When I am designing my own interiors, especially at Stonefields, I try to recapture that play of light and deep shade, using dramatic lighting to highlight jewels I have spent a lifetime collecting.

What do you remember about Kevin and John's original Marnanie flower room?

I had never had a seen a flower room before Marnanie. 'Who dedicates an entire room to flower arranging?' I wondered. Kevin O'Neill, of course, and now me! I can't live in a house without a flower room. I remember it being very functional and slightly devoid of beauty. It had simple timber shelves full of glass and ceramic vases, a basin for water, and a large workbench for arranging. I do remember picking flowers from the garden with Kevin, who only did that as a last resort. He preferred to bring the flowers up from his shop in Melbourne – he hated leaving gaps in the garden beds from harvesting flowers.

How do you use your own flower room?

Our flower room is a multipurpose room used for flower arranging, as a mudroom and for storing and displaying our vast collection of green ceramics. It's the room we enter first when we arrive – all the flowers and plants and food get dumped here, ready for arranging or redistribution. If I had my way again, I would have a room just for flower arranging.

Are there other flower rooms that you've seen in your work or travels which have influenced or inspired you?

I remember visiting Lady Bamford's flower room/potting shed in her estate – Daylesford Farm in the Cotswolds in England. It is very near our precious Garth cottage, so we visit it often. It is highly styled, with an array of vintage terracotta pots on shelves and wicker baskets hanging from the ceiling. What makes it special is the 16th-century stone building it's housed in.

OPPOSITE – *Looking out the doors of the flower room on to the gardens at Stonefields is an endless source of inspiration and joy.*

FOLLOWING – *Paul Bangay's flower room.*

CHAPTER 07 — WORKING WITH FLOWERS AND GREENERY

CASE STUDY

Flower Room at Marnanie

My own flower room at our home, Marnanie, was created from a series of old, dingy, unused rooms that were transformed into a space brimming with peace and serenity. The design began with a piece of furniture that had sentimental meaning for me but was challenging in size and scale. I had definite ideas for the design, so I didn't use an architect. I worked from a stack of images from reference books and old magazines, as well as photographs I had taken over the years.

VISION

For me, the ultimate flower room is a multifunctional space. It connects the interior to the outside world, but also stores gumboots, vintage picnic baskets and unsightly school bags with neon flashing trinkets hanging off them. It shows off newly arrived flowers, greenery and plaited garlic from my vegetable garden. It gleams with copper pots and antique silver champagne buckets, but hides ugly washing machines, plastic mops and tennis bags.

Pleasingly deep drawers hold perfectly pressed collections of monogrammed antique linen napkins. New and old patterned tablecloths from faraway lands. Sets of Georgian cutlery. Shelves filled with beautiful vases and vessels.

There is underfloor heating and huge slabs of stone flooring that make it easy to clean up spills. Deep Belfast sinks with beautiful high English-made taps, and a hose for filling tall vases with water.

A freestanding island bench sits at its centre. Perfect for the arrival of shopping, folding linen, sorting washing or dumping an armful of freshly picked flowers awaiting vases. It is an inspirational space with sensible storage.

OPPOSITE AND FOLLOWING — *My flower room at Marnanie, bursting with delights from the garden and the market.*

CHAPTER 07 – WORKING WITH FLOWERS AND GREENERY

CHALLENGE

The space I was working with was not symmetrical. Without deviating from the original footprint, we demolished three small rooms to create one larger room. We poured a new slab and installed underfloor heating. I chose limestone pavers because I thought it would be interesting to bring an exterior material inside, for both its texture and durability in what would probably be a messy, busy workspace. It also reminded me of the flooring in the 18th-century home I grew up in Ireland.

The walls of this new room were not parallel. To combat this, we laid the flagstones on the diagonal, which purposely drew the eye away from this inherited flaw, as the lines of the pavers and the walls would never be in the same direction. The diagonal lines happily offset the many vertical and horizontal lines within the space.

There was an awkward, unused void that we considered turning into a cellar, walk-in fridge or additional pantry. Instead, with the addition of underfloor heating and a hydronic heater, it became a perfect drying room.

HERO

The hero piece of furniture – a beautiful, generous butcher's block, handmade from hardwood – was designed and manufactured by my father for the kitchen in our home in Ireland. It anchors the space and creates flow of movement as well as being an additional large work surface. It also evokes precious childhood memories of delicious meals, laughter and good times.

Once the butcher's block was in place, I wrapped the room with joinery painted in 'Cabbage Pont' from Resene Paints, which reminded me of the lush garden outside. The room only had one small, off-centre window, so we installed an exact copy to let in more light and create symmetry. Between the windows, I designed a feature splashback in Pentelikon marble – fresh white stone with a slightly green vein that made a subtle nod to the joinery colour – which was also used for the benchtops.

CHARM

During the demolition phase, I noticed that the builders had removed the old outdoor lavatory door and put it on a burn pile on our property. With great difficulty, I carried it 500 metres back to the house. I would repurpose this charming piece as the door to my new drying room. It was hardwood and had original character and stories to tell – perhaps it would swap stories with the butcher's block at night while we all slept.

We also reclaimed doors from a client's old home to use on the powder room and the flower room itself. None of the doors at Marnanie match, so this really worked with the charming through-the-ages aesthetic that had been going on since the house was originally built in 1890.

BESPOKE

Creating a bespoke or customised piece adds authenticity to an interior. I love working with local artisans and manufacturers, partly because I like having creative control, but also because I enjoy collaborating with people who are highly trained in their unique area. It's great to support Australian small businesses and it's better for the environment as the distances between the manufacturer and the site are much shorter!

My flower room had too much white ceiling and I knew it needed something to fill that space. Normally something like an oversized pendant light would work, but the ceiling wasn't high enough. Instead, I collaborated with a talented local to design a rack to hold my copper pots, plaited garlic and dried flowers.

The pot rack had to be beautiful as well as practical and functional. It was made from black steel, which worked well with the antique bronze wall light. I wanted a seamless look with no brackets, so we designed the arms to be fixed behind the ceiling, even though it meant ripping up the floorboards upstairs to bolt it in place. It took the local metalworker who created it, Charlie Aquilina, and builder Jarrod Cowan an entire working day to install. Bespoke hooks for the pots were the finishing touch.

OPPOSITE – *There is charm in the simplicity of the copper pots, antique butcher's block and green joinery.*

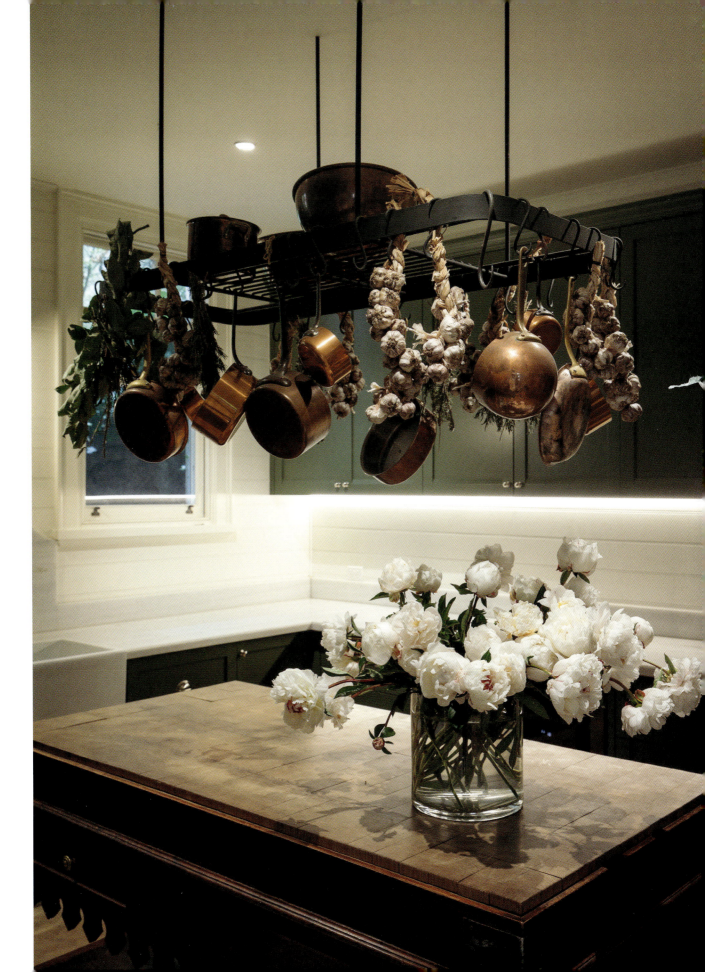

CHAPTER 07 — WORKING WITH FLOWERS AND GREENERY

HOMEGROWN

Marnanie is 740 metres above sea level, so I have had many hits and misses with my beloved vegetable garden. One thing I am proudly self-sufficient in is organic garlic. I wanted to hang my garlic to dry where I could both see it and access it easily for cooking. I like having something grown in abundance on the property both on display and used in the kitchen.

FINAL TOUCH

To finish the room, I created a hat wall to bring in more texture, colour and a sense of story. It holds everything from the old riding hat I wore when I hunted with the Fermanagh Harriers in Ireland to the Akubra hat that my husband, Geordie, wore when he was a 19-year-old jackaroo in outback Australia.

OPPOSITE AND ABOVE — *My flower room can look entirely different depending on the day, and serves many different purposes for my family.*

CHAPTER 07 – WORKING WITH FLOWERS AND GREENERY

How to Make a Flower Room

STEP 1

MAKE A PLAN

Failing to plan is planning to fail! Make a list of all the wonderful and not-so-wonderful objects you want to put in your flower room. Include EVERYTHING from dog food to laundry powder, plastic watering cans to placemats.

STEP 2

REPURPOSE EXISTING PIECES

If you have interesting lighting, artwork or furniture (for example, an antique dresser or island bench) that could find a new life in this room, add them to your list.

STEP 3

DESIGN AND CURATE YOUR SPACE

Design a space for everything on your list. Measure your items and then create cupboards, shelves and drawers to hold them. Start with the biggest items – your washing machine, fridge or dresser – and work around them. Function and practicality are just as important as form. Some essential items, like your vacuum cleaner and mop, will probably need to be stored away so they don't clash with your perfectly selected colour palette but you can give away anything you no longer use or that doesn't bring you joy. Make sure to cull them immediately, otherwise you may find that they are still hanging around a year later.

OPPOSITE – *As Paul Bangay demonstrates here, storage and functionality should be key considerations in a flower room. There is something very pleasing about having the perfect space for every boot, vase and coat.*

Art Credits

37 Cathy Carter, *Icebergs 2018*, 2018, Inkjet print on Fujitrans film, 70 x 60 cm; **72, 93** *Egg prints*, artist unknown; **74** Artist unknown; **75** Two artworks by Elyse Ashe Lord (b. 1900–1971); **85** (clockwise from top left) Barry Humphries, *Shire Beach Mornington*, oil on canvas on board, 46 x 60 cm; Gerrard Lants, *Untitled*; Joseph Milon, *Jeune femme près du basin*; Antonio Pezzella, Positano; David Boyd, *Children in the Fruit Tree*, oil on board; **93** (bottom) Lucy Boyd, *Spring, Paretaio*, 2016, oil on board, 10.2 x 16 cm; **96** Clients own photography; **101** (left wall) A rare set of four finely hand-coloured aquatint plates engraved by G Hunt after original drawings by Lieutenant Joseph Moore, a senior officer of the 89th Regiment, published in 1825 by Kingsbury & Co., London; **131** Collection of hand-engraved 'Fish Series' dinner plates by Johnson Bros England (c. 1961); **135** Inherited antique artwork; **146** Charley Harper, *Tufted Titmouse*, 1954, silkscreen print, 38 x 51 cm; **155** Luke Sciberras, *Portsea*, oil on board; **156** John Brock, Uluru Summer Twilight, 1989, oil on canvas, 81 x 96 cm; **161** Kathleen Ngale, *unknown*, synthetic polymer paint on Belgian linen, 90 x 151 cm; **172** Paul Colin, *Vichy / Demandez Votre Quart*, 1948, lithograph in colours, backed on linen, 160 x 110 cm; **181** Graham Fransella, *Running Figure*, 1990, etching ed. 10/25, 45 x 36 cm; **197** Antique botanical prints, artist unknown; plates and vase by Astier De Villatte, various collections; **199** (clockwise from top left) Vintage pumpkin print purchased at Oak Lane & Co., Kyneton; signed photograph of Queen Elizabeth, inherited, details unknown; following two artworks unknown; Robert Doble, *Portrait of Georgia Weir*; Robert Doble, Orange; **201** *17th Century Italian School (After) Stag Hunt in Classical Landscape*, oil on canvas, 200 x 301 cm; **218** Artist unknown.

Acknowledgements

TO GEORDIE TAYLOR: I love you and our life together very much. Thank you for supporting my career – the future feels exciting and bright alongside you.

TO MY MOTHER, ANDREA COOTE: Thank you for supporting me through another book. Your never-ending belief in me and my ability, provides huge confidence to follow my dreams. I love you.

TO MY BEAUTIFUL DAUGHTERS SYBIL, FRANCESCA AND DAPHNE: I am so grateful for you and love you all so much. It is a joy to watch your growing passions emerge in your lives.

TO JOHN GRAHAM: You are family to Geordie, the girls and I; we all cherish you in our lives and love you very much.

TO MY INCREDIBLE COOTE & CO. TEAM AND ESPECIALLY TO JESSICA PEISLEY: Thank you for your ongoing hard work, loyalty and help in bringing another book to life.

TO MY WONDERFUL CLIENTS: Thank you for trusting me to create beautiful spaces for you to live in. There is no greater honour.

TO PAUL BANGAY: I value our friendship so much. I am grateful for your endless generosity, inspiration and advice. Thank you.

TO KIRSTEN ABBOTT AND ANNA CARLSSON: Thank you for your incredible vision and trust in this book, and for granting me the opportunity to create it.

TO ALEXANDRA TOLSTOY, SARAH MACGREGOR, LULU LYTLE AND THE SCHUMACHER TEAM: Thank you for your time and insights which have provided such a richness of knowledge for this book.

TO INDIA HICKS: Thank you for your wonderful foreword. The world is lucky to have your generous spirit, wit and talent.

TO RACHEL KIM: I am so happy we found each other. The illustrations you have created for this book are beautiful. Thank you.

TO WENDY LEWIS FROM THE TEXTILE TRUNK: Thank you for letting me access your incredible antique textile and wallpaper collection for this book.

TO ANNA MAY: Thank you for your direction with this book.

TO MY MOTHER AND FATHER-IN-LAW TRISH AND IAN: Thank you all for your ongoing encouragement.

TO MY AUNTY AND UNCLE SHERRIE AND TONY: Thank you for your support and love.

TO ARMELLE HABIB, HEATHER NETTE KING AND CARRIE HAWKER: Thank you for your talent and for being so fun to create photographs with.

TO GLENDA DE FIDDES: Thank you for lending us your exquisite antique chintz collection for this book.

TO MY OLDEST AND DEAREST FRIENDS: You know who you are, you mean the world to me. Thank you for your encouragement and love.

TO MICHAEL BYRNE, THE GARDENERS AND TEAM AT MARNANIE, thank you.

First published in Australia in 2024
by Thames & Hudson Australia
Wurundjeri Country, 132A Gwynne Street
Cremorne, Victoria 3121

First published in the United Kingdom in 2025
by Thames & Hudson Ltd
181a High Holborn
London WC1V 7QX

First published in the United States of America in 2025
by Thames & Hudson Inc.
500 Fifth Avenue
New York, New York 10110

The Flower Room © Thames & Hudson Australia 2024
Modern Floral © Thames & Hudson Australia 2024

Text © Charlotte Coote 2024
Images © copyright remains with the individual copyright holders
Illustrations © Rachel Kim (pp. 46–7, 52, 55, 56–7, 59, 60, 61, 194)

27 26 25 24   5 4 3 2 1

The moral right of the author has been asserted.

All rights reserved. No part of this publication may be reproduced or transmitted in any form or by any means, electronic or mechanical, including photocopy, recording or any other information storage or retrieval system, without prior permission in writing from the publisher.

ISBN 978-1-760-76322-0
ISBN 978-1-760-76479-1 (U.S. edition)

 A catalogue record for this book is available from the National Library of Australia

British Library Cataloguing-in-Publication Data
A catalogue record for this book is available from the British Library

Library of Congress Control Number 2024938068

Every effort has been made to trace accurate ownership of copyrighted text and visual materials used in this book. Errors or omissions will be corrected in subsequent editions, provided notification is sent to the publisher.

Front and back cover images: Armelle Habib
U.S. edition front and back cover images: Armelle Habib
Endpapers: Water colour illustration by Rachel Kim, inspired by the antique textile on p. 98

Design: Ashlea O'Neill | Salt Camp Studio
Editing: Lorna Hendry
Printed and bound in China by 1010 Printing International Limited

Thames & Hudson Australia wishes to acknowledge that Aboriginal and Torres Strait Islander peoples are the first storytellers of this nation and the Traditional Custodians of the land on which we live and work.
We acknowledge their continuing culture and pay respect to Elders past and present.

Be the first to know about our new releases, exclusive content and author events by visiting
thamesandhudson.com.au
thamesandhudson.com
thamesandhudsonusa.com

Photography credits

Armelle Habib
pp. 1, 8, 10–11, 13, 14, 17, 18, 34, 36, 37, 41, 42, 45, 64, 67, 68, 70–1, 72, 75, 76, 78, 79, 80, 83, 84, 85, 86–7, 88, 90–1, 92, 93, 94, 96, 97, 101, 104, 105, 106–07, 108–09, 110–11, 114, 118, 120, 122–3, 124, 125, 126, 127, 128–9, 130, 131, 132, 133, 138–9, 140, 141, 142–3, 144–5, 146, 147, 148, 149, 150, 151, 152, 153, 154–5, 156, 157, 158–9, 160, 162–3, 164, 165, 169, 170, 172, 173, 174–5, 176, 177 (clockwise from top left, image 1, 3 & 4), 178, 179, 180, 181, 182, 183, 186 (clockwise from top left, image 1 & 2), 187, 188, 192, 195, 200, 201, 202, 206, 209, 210–1, 212, 214–5, 219, 220, 222

Marcel Aucar
pp. 135, 136, 161, 217, 218

Lisa Cohen
pp. 7, 74, 102, 117, 119, 177 (clockwise from top left, image 2), 191, 198, 203, 204–5

Sarah Pannell
p. 12

Hannah Puechmarin
pp. 77, 82, 134, 137, 184–5, 186 (clockwise from top left, image 3 & 4)

Abbie Mellé
pp. 136, 196, 197, 199

Charlotte Coote
pp. 20–33, 89

Boz Gagovski
p. 112